BRAD JOHNSON

PLAY WITH PASSION

Positively for Kids®
811 Kirkland Avenue, Suite 200
Kirkland, WA 98033
www.positivelyforkids.com

Johnson, Brad, 1968-
Brad Johnson—Play with Passion/ by Brad Johnson with Greg Brown
48-p.:ill. (mostly col.), ports.; 26 cm (...series...)
Summary: Describes the life of Brad Johnson, quarterback for the Super Bowl winning
Tampa Bay Buccaneers, and presents his belief that having passion is essential to any
kind of success.
Audience: Grades 4-8

ISBN 0-9634650-4-x

I. Johnson, Brad, 1968- Juvenile literature. 2. Football players—United States—
Biography—Juvenile literature. [I. Johnson, Brad, 1968-. 2. Football Players—Biography]
I. Brown, Greg, 1957-. II. Title.

796.332/092—dc21[B]

Library of Congress Control Number:
2004091247

Photo Credits:
All photos courtesy of Brad Johnson and family except the following:
AP/Wide World: 28 middle; 30 right; 32 top left; 32 middle left; 34 left; 35 left; 35 right;
39 bottom left; 39 bottom right; 40 top right; 41 middle; 45. Bob Washel: 40 top left;
40 bottom right; 41 left; 41 right. *Black Mountain News*: 40 bottom left. Getty Images: 3;
14 right; 19; 43 top left. Tampa Bay Buccaneers: 5 right. *Tampa Bay Tribune*: 43 bottom.
Timothy A. Clary/AFP/Getty Images: cover. Tom Dipace: 6; 28 left; 29; 30 left; 32 top
right; 32 bottom right; 32 bottom left; 36; 37; 39 top; 43 top right; 46.

Special Thanks:
Positively For Kids would like to thank the people and organizations that helped make
this book possible: Brad Johnson, his wife Nikki, and his parents Ellen and Rick
Johnson; Brian Lammi of Lammi Sports Management; the Tampa Bay Buccaneers;
and the Glazer Family Foundation.

Book Design:
Methodologie, Inc., Seattle

Printed in Canada

BRAD JOHNSON

PLAY WITH PASSION

BY BRAD JOHNSON
WITH GREG BROWN

A POSITIVELY FOR KIDS BOOK

Hi! I'm Brad Johnson.

My journey through the National Football League has had many delays and detours.

After 11 years in the league, I finally crossed paths with greatness by playing in the 2003 Super Bowl and helping Tampa Bay demolish Oakland 48-21.

Nobody's life is a smooth ride to success. Mine certainly hasn't been. I never accomplished my childhood dream. I never played on an All-Star football team in high school or college. My pro career started with a crawl. I didn't throw a single touchdown in my first four seasons in the NFL. Unlucky injuries plagued me. I even injured my neck—while sleeping!

As I look back on my travels from small town Black Mountain, North Carolina, to Super Bowl Sunday I can't believe all the turns.

So how did I do it? You have to have passion.

The passion I'm talking about isn't the hoopla that happens when our team scores a touchdown.

Dan, Great To Meet You!

Brad Johnson
14

YEAR 1979

YEAR 2003

BUCCANEERS

Jumping up and down and screaming on a field is easy. Anyone can do that.

Sure, I like celebrating as much as anyone. What I'm talking about, however, is the quiet, burning internal drive that gets your heart pumping.

What's your passion? What's the one thing you love to do the most? What are your goals? Either you are moving forward or you're not. One of the saddest things is going through life passionless.

Having passion means you can't wait to get out of bed. It means you're fired up to set goals and reach for them, even though you might fail.

It means you're willing to work towards something, willing to give up other things to get it. It means pushing through the pain of preparation.

It means standing strong and not giving up, even when you're hurt and run into what seems like a dead end. It's all about surviving and thriving.

Winning a Super Bowl doesn't mean I have all the answers. But my hope is that the true stories in this book will help you apply the power of passion to your life.

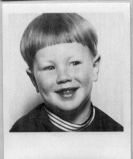

> In these pictures I'm proudly posing—with a guitar, with my newborn sister on the couch next to Mom, with my new bike on my fourth birthday, in my school picture, and with a bat in front of Dad's car.

My parents, Ellen and Rick, were into sports and both loved basketball. Both played sports and started their careers as physical education teachers. Mom played high school basketball and helped her team win a state title. Dad coached high school basketball.

On Friday the 13th, September, 1968, my father heard about my birth while coaching a high school basketball game. Everyone in the gym stood up and cheered an announcement that proclaimed Coach Johnson had a son. My grandmother heard about my birth while listening to the game on the radio.

So it was no surprise to anyone when my parents bought a plastic hoop and put a foam basketball in my hands as soon as I could walk.

The hoop fit on the back of a chair and had a bell. Every time the ball fell through the rim, it rang. Although I don't remember it, my parents say I loved making that bell ring. Over and over. For hours.

"Knee football" is the first game I ever played. Dad and I made the living room carpet a football field. I got four downs to run the football the length of our couch. Dad would play from his hands and knees. Sometimes he let me win, sometimes not.

We played all sorts of games that improved my sports skills. Dad always made it fun. For example, in high school, he devised a two-person football game in our yard where he'd rush me and I'd try to throw passes to trees. If I hit the tree trunk it counted as a completion.

You could say I was an active child. I didn't sit around and watch much TV. I wanted to be out doing things. Throughout my sports career I've had my share of broken bones—collar, ankle, fingers, and neck. I broke my first bone at age 4. I fell down steps at a neighbor's house. Mom said it was the first time she ever saw an arm shaped like an S.

My other childhood injury happened at age 5. Dad had a passion for golf. One day he wanted to practice his chipping in our yard. So he told me to hold a stick and warned me not to move, no matter what.

Dad backed up about 100 yards and figured he'd never hit the ball close to me or the stick. One shot arced high above our trees and headed right toward me. I froze.

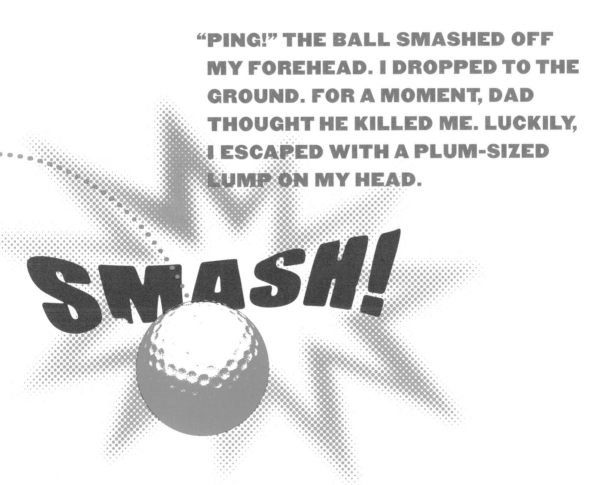

"PING!" THE BALL SMASHED OFF MY FOREHEAD. I DROPPED TO THE GROUND. FOR A MOMENT, DAD THOUGHT HE KILLED ME. LUCKILY, I ESCAPED WITH A PLUM-SIZED LUMP ON MY HEAD.

SMASH!

Black Mountain, NC
Toronto
Detroit
Toledo
Roch
ester
Buffalo
Cleveland
IND
OHIO
Columbus
Cincinnati
PA
Pittsburgh
Harrisburg
Baltimore
Charleston
Washington
Richmond
VA.
NC
Raleigh
SC
Columbia
Charleston
Augusta
Savannah
Jacksonville
FLA
GA
PPALACHIAN MTS
Albany
MASS
CONN
Concord
Boston
Providence
New York
Trenton
Philadelphia
DEL
C Hatteras

Despite my run-in with a golf ball, it didn't leave any lasting fears. I love playing golf now. Not much scared me growing up. I could handle the darkness of our secluded home on a hill near the small town of Black Mountain, North Carolina. I could handle scary movies. There is one thing that is my kryptonite, even today.

What gives me the willies and makes me weak is—ketchup. I can't stand the smell. The taste gags me. I can't handle a bottle close to me. I always demand "no ketchup" on my hamburgers. I check under the bun of every hamburger to make sure.

In college, friends would try to sneak the sauce on my food when I wasn't looking. My nose always saved me.

WHEN I WAS A KID, MY BEDROOM LEFT LITTLE DOUBT I LOVED SPORTS. EVERY INCH OF MY WALLS WAS COVERED WITH POSTERS OF MY FAVORITE ATHLETES OR MOTIVATIONAL SAYINGS. LARRY BIRD, MAGIC JOHNSON, TERRY BRADSHAW, WARREN MOON, AND DAN FOUTS WERE ON MY WALLS.

I hand-painted inspirational phrases near my posters. One of my favorites to this day is: "It's good to have an end to journey towards, but it's the journey that matters in the end."

> This family Christmas picture shows one of my prized possessions—my Washington Redskins leather jacket.

In elementary school, I slept with my baseball mitt next to my pillow and dreamed of playing for the Yankees. I wore a leather Washington Redskins jacket and pictured myself in the NFL. I even had a Washington Redskins light switch. But basketball is what turned me on the most. Playing big-time college basketball and then going to the NBA became my goal.

School turned me off, at first. My parents held me back a year, so I attended first grade twice. It was one of the best things my parents did for me.

My first try at first grade I had the worst test scores of the class. I felt embarrassed to raise my hand and kept inside my shy shell.

One day on my bus ride home, kids blocked the aisle when it was my turn to get off. So instead of asking them to move, I just sat in the back. I didn't want to speak up for myself. I stayed in the back until everyone got off.

The bus driver found me in the back sniffling and kindly drove me home.

> Julie and I smile for the camera.

> The totem pole picture was
taken at Camp Ridgecrest with
my parents. I was 5 years old.

The next year I changed schools and visited an after-school tutor. I understood
the lessons and gained confidence. I just needed a little extra time. I came out of
my shell and wasn't afraid to ask questions anymore.

As I continued through school, I wasn't the smartest in my class. I worked
hard to keep up. I finished high school with a 3.3 grade average and was voted
Class President my senior year.

Sports helped me feel good about myself, too. I wore my Redskins jacket to
elementary school. It had bright yellow sleeves and a sharp red vest. Sometimes
I let girls wear it for a day.

By the time I was in sixth grade, I discovered big-brother responsibility. My
younger sister, Julie, my only sibling, started school. Our school bus dropped us
off at the bottom of our hill. We walked a half-mile up our steep gravel road every
day. To Julie, it seemed we were climbing Mount Everest. I'd carry her school
bags. I'd coax her. I'd encourage her. We'd take breaks. About three-quarters of
the way up, we'd stop at a neighbor's house for a water break. It got old, but I
never left her behind. Somehow we made it up our hill every day.

On the playfield I felt responsibility for winning. I grew up being one of the
bigger kids in my class. During recess, whenever we picked teams for kickball,

basketball, or capture the flag, captains would choose me first because my teams usually won.

I always felt sorry for the kids who were picked last. So one day, when I was a captain, I picked a girl who wasn't a very good athlete with my first pick. Everyone was stunned. Then I picked her best friend. They both jumped up and down with delight. It made me feel good inside.

The girl appreciated it so much she helped me in school. Don't let your passion blind your compassion. Plenty of people have shown me compassion.

During the summer months, Dad directed a summer camp, just two miles away from our house. I attended every year along with 200 other kids. There were crafts, competitions, sports, and traditions.

When someone had a birthday, the whole camp would sing "Happy Birthday" and then adults took the birthday boy to the dock and threw him in the lake. My birthday is in September, well after the summer camp. So when I turned 6, my parents woke me up at 6 in the morning and said, "In the lake!" I jumped in the chilly water. It sounds mean, but it was a joke that makes me laugh whenever I think about it.

It's a reminder to never take yourself too seriously.

← **16 feet** →

> I'm guessing I was about 9 or 10 in both these pictures. Looks like I was getting a little too big for my baseball uniform.

World-record-length banana splits were another camp tradition. Long gutters, lined with foil, were filled with ice cream, toppings, and bananas. The campers feasted free-for-all style with their hands.

FOR MY 16TH BIRTHDAY, MY PARENTS MADE A 16-FOOT BANANA SPLIT, AND WE INVITED MY HIGH SCHOOL FOOTBALL TEAM AND THE CHEERLEADERS TO HELP EAT IT.

Capture the flag and sock wars were favorite camp activities. But four square with a rubber ball was the best game of all. And with so many kids, someone always wanted to play. If I could beat those in my age group, I'd play guys older than me. Playing against tough competition made me better.

My heart wasn't into my first few seasons of tackle football. I played mostly to be with friends. I started at age 6 and played offensive line, being the big kid.

I had one tiny problem. I hated blocking and tackling. I accidentally broke a teammate's leg during practice, which made me timid because I didn't want to hurt anyone.

Eventually, coaches noticed I could throw the football. I didn't know much about the quarterback position. I could throw rocks well. I pitched in Little League, so I knew I had a good arm.

Two people, Coach Minnick and Coach Silvers saw a quarterback inside me and convinced me to try the position. They worked with me during the summer. While I was in elementary school they gave me the quarterback job.

That first year I threw many interceptions and we lost some games because of me. Thing is, we kept throwing the ball.

Coach Minnick saw my potential. He kept encouraging me, as did my parents. I took losing so hard, however, Coach Minnick came to my house after some games just to tell me "Tomorrow's another day" and give me a pat on the back.

My coaches would tell me, "Be at practice tomorrow." They didn't give up on me. Passion without encouragement dries like water in a desert.

Being a quarterback got me interested in punt, pass, and kick competitions. Kids ages 8–13 from all over the country compete. The national championships are held at the halftime of an NFL game.

Dad helped me practice all three skills. My goal was to win a state title and compete at an Atlanta Falcons game. I tried two years and never accomplished my goal.

One year I needed a pressure punt to make the state competition, and I nailed it to qualify. That was my greatest comeback as a kid.

Competing against guys from all over the state taught me to look beyond the borders of our town. It showed me there were many athletes better than myself out there. That motivated me. I knew I'd never be the fastest or strongest athlete. My goal was to work the hardest. Dad used to tell me that to succeed I needed to practice when others my age weren't.

I still loved basketball the most, so every day I came home from school and shot baskets. I'd shovel snow off our gravel road in the winter to practice. But a lot of kids do that.

> Here are two pictures of Dad and me. Dad coached my basketball team in seventh grade (I'm on the far right in the back).

> Dad is next to me in this newspaper clipping after I won a local Punt, Pass and Kick contest.

Punt, Pass And Kick Champ

ohnson (right) demon- Ntor Co. Observing Brad are (L-R), fifth-grader at Black Mountain
s passing ability which Lroy Robinson, president of dle School, will compete for th
Milhouse in Asheville, Larry Grant trict title in Charlotte later

MY ALL-TIME FAVORITE TIME TO SHOOT HOOPS OUTSIDE WAS IN THE RAIN. I LOVED GETTING DRENCHED. THAT'S BECAUSE I KNEW NOBODY ELSE IN MY AREA WOULD BE SHOOTING HOOPS IN THE RAIN.

So I'd shoot baskets at night—sometimes in the middle of the night, if I couldn't sleep. Mom or Julie often came outside and rebounded for me.

As I got older and could drive, I'd go to school at 6 in the morning and practice by myself before school. Sometimes after dates in high school, I'd go shoot hoops in the gym.

I'd go on early-morning 10-mile runs a few times a week. I'd even practice punishment drills coaches used. In basketball everyone dreaded "the worm" drill. Football had "the bear crawl." I'd practice those on my own so when we did them in school practice they didn't seem so painful.

While my parents supported me in sports, they always wanted me to be well-rounded. One year they bought me a trumpet. I immediately set a goal of being first chair in the school band. I made first chair by default.

The best trumpet player stayed up most of the night before the tryouts. He couldn't make a sound the next day because his lips were swollen, proving there is such a thing as too much practice. I stopped playing the trumpet the next year.

Singing became my musical passion in high school. I wanted to sing at the school talent show. So my senior year I convinced nine friends to help.

Eight girls, dressed in prom dresses, danced beside me as I sat on a throne. The other friend played the piano. I sang "Just a Bowl of Butter Beans."

I WENT ALL OUT, WEARING A WHITE TUX, WITH PINK CUMMER-BUND AND PINK TENNIS SHOES. I WASN'T THE BEST SINGER, SO I KNEW OUR PRESENTATION HAD TO SHOW OUR PASSION. IT DID.

Finishing second proved passion goes a long way to compensate for lack of talent. And even if you are not the best, you can still give it your best.

BRAD'S HIGH SCHOOL ACHIEVEMENTS 1984-87

Football	Basketball
5,031 total yards passing	2,392 total points
Four-year letterman	Four-year letterman
All-State his senior year	All-State his senior year
All-America Quarterback	Western N.C. Player of the Year
Western N.C. Player of the Year	

> My senior year I went with the curly look.

My first high school football game proved humbling. I became the first ninth-grader at Owen High to start at quarterback for the Warhorses.

There were great expectations for "Big Bad Brad," as they used to call me. I had a respectable showing, completing 8 of 12 passes with two interceptions. We lost to our rival, but I felt good about my game. The next day we had practice and some teammates were reading the newspaper about our game. A teammate read aloud, "Brad Johnson looked erratic."

"ERRATIC?"
I SAID, THINKING THAT WAS A GOOD THING.
"YEAH, I WAS ERRATIC. I PUT ON A SHOW!"
MY TEAMMATES LAUGHED AT MY MISTAKE.

Convincing my senior teammates to respect and believe in a ninth grader became my toughest challenge. There were times in the huddle when the older guys just didn't want to listen to me. Even though we were 5-5 that season, my love for the game won respect. When you show passion, it can turn doubters into believers.

> Listening to instructions from Coach Franklin Cecil, along with teammate Paul Moore, during my sophomore season.

> Posing in my freshman year.

> Our annual senior photo in front of our high school field with Coach Kenny Ford.

People might think because I'm an NFL quarterback that everything went my way in high school. That's just not true. Throughout my four seasons I had memorable games and ones I'd rather forget.

One of my worst games came my senior year with a college coach from Florida State University in the stands watching. My stats were terrible with four interceptions. I thought I blew my chance at a college scholarship. After one tough loss, the opponents' cheerleaders mockingly sang "Happy Birthday" to me as I walked in the parking lot to my car.

In one of my best comebacks, I threw two interceptions in the first half and our team trailed by a couple touchdowns. My coach yelled his head off at us in the halftime locker room. In the second half, I threw two touchdowns and ran for another in our victory.

A trick play we called "The Whammy" still is my favorite high school moment. We were small-school underdogs to big-school Reynolds High my senior year. We seniors were especially motivated as we had lost to Reynolds three straight times. We used "The Whammy" on our first play.

After we returned the opening kickoff to the 25-yard line and referees stopped play, I knelt down next to the ball and pretended to tie my shoe. My teammates jogged to the far sideline pretending to leave the field. They suddenly stopped and lined up away from the ball. I picked up the ball and passed it across the field. Our receiver caught it and raced down the sidelines untouched for a score.

Shaken, a Reynolds player fumbled the kickoff and we recovered. I tossed a TD pass on our next play. Up 14-0 after two plays, we defeated Reynolds.

$1 AN HOUR

Throughout high school I worked for one man—George Pickering. I did odd jobs for him—sweeping floors, setting up tables, and yard work. He paid me $1 an hour. Sometimes I'd work the whole weekend and make $25. Mr. Pickering also made a bet with me. He promised to pay me $200 if I went through high school without drinking alcohol. That wasn't hard. I didn't go to parties and didn't drink anyway. After I graduated he gave me $500.

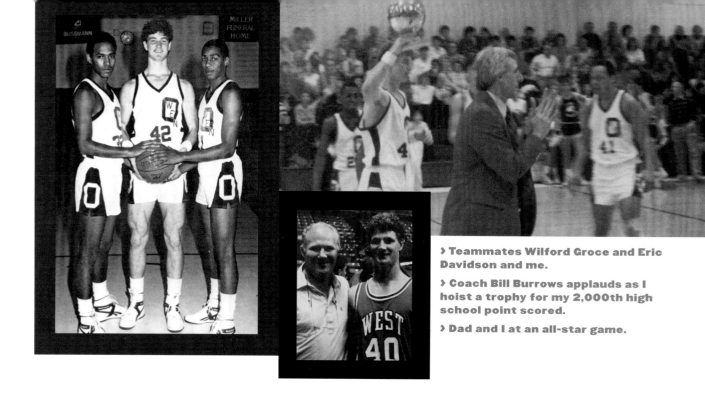

> Teammates Wilford Groce and Eric Davidson and me.

> Coach Bill Burrows applauds as I hoist a trophy for my 2,000th high school point scored.

> Dad and I at an all-star game.

The ultimate goal in high school is to win a state championship. I wasn't able to experience that in football or basketball. We came closest in basketball.

I scored 2,392 points in high school. Sometimes I made the game-winning shot, sometimes I missed it. One game, my best friend fouled me in the final seconds with our team trailing by a point. I made both free throws for the victory.

In a quarterfinal state playoff game my junior year, I missed a shot from close range in the final seconds that would have won the game.

THAT NIGHT I SAT IN OUR KITCHEN FOR HOURS THINKING ABOUT THAT LAST PLAY.

During my first two basketball seasons, I found myself tired and missing shots at the end of games. Dad and I had long talks about why.

We decided I needed to practice differently and work harder on my conditioning. I vowed I'd be the best-conditioned athlete around.

I ran more—up and down hills, 2 to 4 miles before school. I did whatever it took to be in great shape. I created pressure situations for myself when I practiced on my own.

For example, when shooting free throws, for every shot missed I'd force myself to run extra. That way I practiced shooting with pressure.

My senior year I made some key baskets at the end of games thanks to my pressure practices.

FUN FACT >>> BRAD STOOD 6-FOOT-3 AS A FRESHMAN IN HIGH SCHOOL. HE MAXED OUT AT 6-5.

That year we made it to the North Carolina state tournament semifinals before losing. I felt I let Mom down because she had won a state basketball title.

"I'm sorry I let you down," I told her. "I'm sorry I didn't make your goals."

Mom gave me a hug and said it was silly of me to think that way. She told me how proud she was of my hard work and all my accomplishments. The state title didn't matter, she said.

DURING MY SENIOR BASKETBALL SEASON, I ACCEPTED A FOOTBALL SCHOLARSHIP TO FLORIDA STATE UNIVERSITY. I DECIDED ON FSU FOR MANY REASONS. THEY PROMISED I COULD PLAY FOOTBALL AND BASKETBALL.

Knowing my college would be paid, I decided to use money I won for scholar-athlete awards (about $1,000) to create a fund for our school's teachers. That fund continues today and gives recognition each year to a teacher voted most inspirational by the athletes.

It was my way of saying thank you to the teachers and coaches who educated me.

FLORIDA STATE UNIVERSITY

Brad Passing

Year	Att	Comp	Pct	Yards	TD	Int
'88	13	8	.615	81	1	1
'89	12	7	.883	67	0	0
'90	163	109	.669	1,136	8	5
'91	61	37	.607	462	5	3
Totals	249	161	.646	1,746	14	9

My freshman year I did realize my dream of playing college basketball. I started two FSU games. I created a problem for our coach.

The guy whose starting spot I took was a senior. He waited five years to start. I could see the demotion hurt him and our team unity. So I went to my coach and asked him to bench me. He did. I came off the bench the rest of the season.

As a player, you have to put the team's needs ahead of your own.

My first year of football at FSU I didn't play a single down because I red-shirted (which means you practice but don't play in games). My freshman and sophomore years I played a few times but spent most games on the sidelines, waiting my turn.

College basketball made me realize I probably wouldn't play in the NBA. So I decided to focus on football. I worked out harder than ever. Each of my four years I earned "best conditioned athlete" on the team.

I got the chance I dreamed about my junior year—starting six games, winning four. Unfortunately, Coach Bobby Bowden replaced me with fellow quarterback Casey Weldon the rest of the year. I knew how much Casey wanted to play because I wanted it just as much. I congratulated him after victories, but it hurt standing on the sidelines.

I felt like quitting. Keeping your passion during success is easy. The true test is when things don't go your way. Can you hold on and stay positive when your dreams seem to be crumbling? There were days I pouted and felt sorry for myself.

> My first day at college I met Casey Weldon, a fellow fresh-man quarterback from Florida. We became fast friends, despite competing for the same position on the field.

> Shooting from the outside at FSU game.

> I pause for a break during a trip down the Colorado River my junior year in college. Alex Serrano and I get to work in the weightroom.

About that time I met a sports psychologist, Alex Serrano. He saw my potential and helped me train differently. Instead of power lifting and running for endurance, he created drills specifically for a quarterback. I ran in the sand and did drills that made my teammates tease me.

I kept working hard. Alex also helped with my mental outlook. Critics claimed my foot speed was too slow. Alex helped me believe "I am fast enough to get the job done."

I played sparingly my senior year and started thinking I would never play again. Casey shined that season and was the 1991 Heisman Trophy runner-up. Deep down I knew I could play, but I just wasn't given the chance. Banging my head against a wall would have hurt less.

So you can imagine my surprise when Dad and I heard my name announced on TV during the NFL draft.

WE WERE IN MY COLLEGE DORM ROOM WHEN THE MINNESOTA VIKINGS PICKED ME IN THE NINTH ROUND. CASEY WENT TO PHILADELPHIA IN THE THIRD, ONLY THE SECOND TIME TWO QUARTERBACKS FROM THE SAME TEAM HAD BEEN DRAFTED IN THE SAME YEAR.

FUN FACT >>> ONE SUMMER AT FSU, BRAD WORKED AT NABISCO® IN THE TRUCK LOADING/UNLOADING DEPARTMENT. HE MOVED BOXES OF WHEAT THINS® AND OREO® COOKIES FOR $7 AN HOUR.

27

IN MINNESOTA, TWO THINGS SURPRISED ME —HOW TALENTED NFL ATHLETES ARE AND HOW HARD THEY WORK. THE EXTENSIVE GAME PLANS ALSO IMPRESSED ME. IN COLLEGE, WE MIGHT HAVE ONE PASS ROUTE CALLED A CURL. THE NFL HAS 10 WAYS TO RUN A CURL.

Just making the team as a rookie made me feel I reached a goal. I didn't play a single down my first two years in the NFL. Again I played the waiting game.

After playing in just three games my third year, I asked the Vikings to let me play in Europe. I needed experience. I was willing to do what's necessary to succeed. I'd go anywhere. So I played for the World League's London Monarchs. I gained confidence by leading the league in completions and throwing 13 touchdowns.

I entered the 1995 season ready to play. Once again I saw limited duty as the backup to Warren Moon, one of my childhood heroes. After four seasons I still did not have an NFL touchdown pass.

I won the starting job the next season and threw my first TD pass in the first game. It was special because Dad, recovering from a heart operation, was in the stands. As I walked off the field, I tossed him the touchdown ball. That was my way of saluting him for all he had done for me. I played in a dozen games that year and started to make a name for myself.

> Watching from the sidelines with the Vikings.

> Leading the London Monarchs.

> Enjoying time with my dad.

28

Injuries marred the next two seasons. Whenever I took a step forward, it seemed I'd have to take two steps back.

Everything went my way the first 12 games of 1997. We were winning, and the ball bounced our way. I even threw an NFL first—a touchdown pass to myself (I caught a deflected pass and carried it in for a TD from 3 yards out).

DURING THE 13TH WEEK, HOWEVER, I INJURED MY NECK SLEEPING. IT SOUNDS WEIRD, BUT IT'S TRUE.

The night before our Monday Night Football game with Green Bay, I woke up with a sore, stiff neck. I played despite the pain and inability to grip the ball. After the game, X-rays showed I fractured a neck bone and needed surgery. I missed the rest of the season and a playoff run.

A broken leg and broken right thumb limited my playing time to just four games in 1998. Randall Cunningham revived his career while I was down and that made me expendable.

JUST MARRIED

I enjoyed my time in Minnesota. I met many great friends. Most important, however, during that time I met my wife.

Back in college my quarterback coach Mark Richt always said, "You have to meet my sister." Unfortunately, Nikki played volleyball at the University of South Florida, about a 3 1/2-hour drive away, so we didn't meet in college.

After my first year with the Vikings, Mark got us together for one date. We liked each other, but nothing happened between us, no passion.

Four years passed. In the off-season I lived in Tallahassee. I'd run into Mark and ask, "How's your sister doing?"

One weekend, Nikki visited Mark, so he hooked us up again. This time, we both felt an attraction. We started dating long distance. A year later we were married in 1999.

ROCK STAR

I fulfilled a dream by recording a song on a CD. The NFL made a CD called "NFL Country," matching players with singers. I teamed with country recording artist Jo Dee Messina. We sang "I'm a Survivor." The words sum up my

I was born a believer,
biggest dreamer this world has ever seen
Ready to face most anything,
but learned that I was naive
Ran into things in life that I never planned
But that's made me who I am
I've had highs and lows and seen my share
of ups and downs
But I'm still here
Cause I'm a survivor
I won't let it get the best of me,
I'll try my very best to be that strong
Oh, oh, oh, I'm a survivor
And I'll never give up, never lay down,
never give in
I'll just keep moving on.

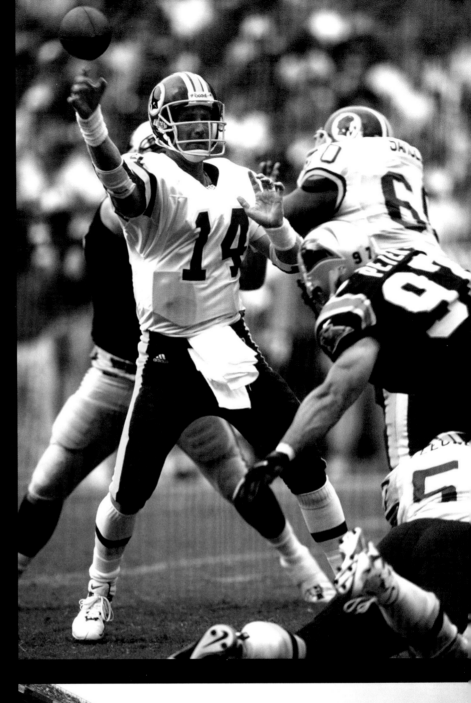

THE WEEK BEFORE I MARRIED NIKKI, **THE VIKINGS TRADED ME TO THE WASHINGTON REDSKINS, MY FAVORITE BOYHOOD TEAM.** THE MOVE REUNITED ME WITH CASEY, MY FORMER FSU TEAMMATE.

This time, however, I earned the starting job and Casey was the backup. The 1999 season seemed magical as we clinched the NFC East title by overcoming a 20-10 fourth-quarter deficit to win 26-20 in overtime. We beat Detroit in the playoffs for Washington's first playoff win in nine years. I felt I showed what I could do in the NFL. I felt proud to play in the Pro Bowl that year—my first All-Star football game.

Expectations soared entering the 2000 season as Washington picked up big-name free agents. But it proved to be a frustrating season for the team and me. I hurt my knee, again on Monday Night Football, and backup Jeff George played most of the season. We failed to make the playoffs.

I became a free agent at the end of the season and signed with Tampa Bay.

BRAD'S CAREER PASSING STATS

Brad Passing

	Year	G	GS	Att	Comp	Pct	Yards	YPA	Lg	TD	Int	Tkld	20+	40+	Rate
Minnesota	'92	0	0	0	0	0	0	0	0	0	0	0	0	0	0
Vikings	'93	0	0	0	0	0	0	0	0	0	0	0	0	0	0
	'94	4	0	37	22	59.5	150	4.05	15	0	0	1/5	0	0	68.5
	'95	5	0	36	25	69.4	272	7.56	39	0	2	2/18	4	0	68.3
	'96	12	8	311	195	62.7	2258	7.26	82	17	10	15/119	27	7	89.4
	'97	13	13	452	275	60.8	3036	6.72	56	20	12	26/164	36	7	84.5
	'98	4	2	101	65	64.4	747	7.40	48	7	5	4/30	7	2	89.0
Washington	'99	16	16	519	316	60.9	4005	7.72	65	24	13	29/177	62	14	90.0
Redskins	'00	12	11	365	228	62.5	2505	6.86	77	11	15	20/150	23	7	75.7
Tampa Bay	'01	16	16	559	340	60.8	3406	6.09	47	13	11	44/269	34	1	77.7
Buccaneers	'02	13	13	451	281	62.3	3049	6.76	76	22	6	21/121	32	6	92.9
	'03	16	16	570	354	62.1	3811	6.69	76	26	21	20/111	37	9	81.5
	TOTAL	111	95	3401	2101	61.8	23239	6.83	82	140	95	182/1164	262	53	84.1

RETURNING TO FLORIDA FELT LIKE A HOME-COMING. I ALSO KNEW IT WOULD BE A CHALLENGE. TAMPA BAY HAD NEVER BEEN TO THE SUPER BOWL. THE BUCS HAD NEVER WON A PLAYOFF GAME ON THE ROAD.

Going into a new situation is always tough. Some people try too hard to fit in right away. I came in humble and willing to earn my teammates' respect with patience and hard work.

I won the quarterback job and started all 16 regular-season games. Our crushing defense led the way and our offense didn't make many mistakes. We set a Buccaneers record for fewest interceptions in a season.

But disaster struck in the playoffs. We fell behind in the first half and our offense needed to take risks. I forced some passes and finished with four interceptions in the 31-9 loss to Philadelphia. It's always miserable to end the season with a loss, especially that way.

New coach Jon Gruden set a new tone for the 2002 season. Coach Gruden is a passion builder who leads by example. He has a way of building up his players, and he gets excited!

FUN FACT >>> PLAYING FOOTBALL IN TAMPA BAY'S FALL HEAT TAKES ITS TOLL ON BRAD'S UNIFORM. HE CHANGES HIS JERSEY THREE OR FOUR TIMES A GAME BECAUSE THEY GET SOAKED WITH SWEAT. AT HALFTIME, BRAD CHANGES SHOULDER PADS, SOCKS, AND SHOES.

"MAN, YOU ARE AN ACCURATE PASSER," HE'D SAY TO ME. "I DON'T UNDERSTAND WHY PEOPLE GET ON YOU ABOUT YOUR MOBILITY. YOU'RE MAKING PLAYS."

Players on defense and offense made plays all season. We dominated with a 12-4 record. Our smothering defense received well-deserved credit, and our offense set 10 new team records.

A test for me came in the sixth game when I broke a rib. Every deep breath felt like a knife in my back as it healed. There's not much that can be done for broken ribs. I had to suffer through it. In my very first game back I threw five touchdowns.

Then we got hot in the playoffs, beating San Francisco 31-6 and Philadelphia 27-10.

Against the 49ers I suffered a scare. A defender's finger accidentally poked through my facemask and opened a bloody gash above my eye. A cart took me to the locker room. On the way out I gave the thumbs up to Nikki to let her know I was OK. I did return to play in the second half with eight stitches.

That put us in the NFC championship at chilly Philadelphia up against history. The Eagles were playing their final game at Veterans Stadium.

As crazy as it sounds, the NFC Championship seemed like the Super Bowl to me. This was the biggest step to get to the big game.

The Eagles took the opening kickoff 70 yards and took a 7-0 lead within the first minute. Nobody panicked. We wore them down to earn a trip to San Diego and Super Bowl XXXVIII.

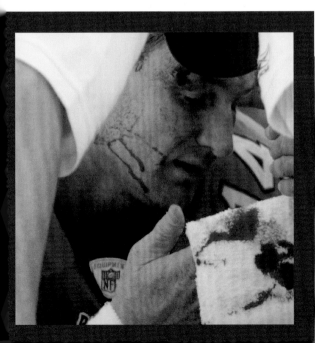

THE NIGHT BEFORE THE SUPER BOWL I COULDN'T SLEEP. AT 1:30 IN THE MORNING I WOKE UP WITH MY HEART POUNDING AS IF I'D BEEN RUNNING. I KEPT TELLING MYSELF "YOU'VE GOT TO GET TO SLEEP." I FINALLY DOZED OFF AT 5:30 A.M.

By game time, I was ready to play and felt relaxed.

There wasn't much dramatic tension in our 27-point victory over the Raiders. Our defense scored 21 points on three of its five interceptions. Offensively, we did our job, too.

Two crucial drives were memorable. We marched 89 yards in 10 plays for a touchdown just before the half to make it 20-3.

Our defense held the Raiders at the start of the second half. We took over and faced a third-and-2 at our 19. Everyone was covered, so I scrambled and ran for 10 yards to keep alive the scoring drive that put us up 27-3.

For all who told me I was too slow, I showed I was fast enough.

After the game, we all felt the pride of our accomplishment. Mostly, we felt unity. It wasn't about any one person; it was about us as a family.

Standing on the field I held my oldest son Max in one arm with my other around Nikki. To be in the winning moment together is what I'll remember most.

I've always watched the game at some party, on some couch, eating chips and dip, and never realized that it might be me one day. You talk about it. You think about it. You work for it. But to be that guy saying, "I'm going to Disney World," to stand there with my wife and son was unreal. For at least one moment I was the No. 1 quarterback in the world on the best team in the world. Awesome!

FUN FACT >>> BRAD WON THE 2003 NFL QUARTERBACK CHALLENGE, BECOMING THE ONLY PLAYER IN NFL HISTORY TO WIN THE SUPER BOWL, PRO BOWL, AND QUARTERBACK CHALLENGE IN THE SAME YEAR.

BRAD'S
SUPER BOWL STATS
TAMPA BAY

	Att.	Comp.	Yds.	TD	Int.
Passing					
B. JOHNSON	34	18	215	2	1
Rushing					
B. JOHNSON	1	10	10	0	–

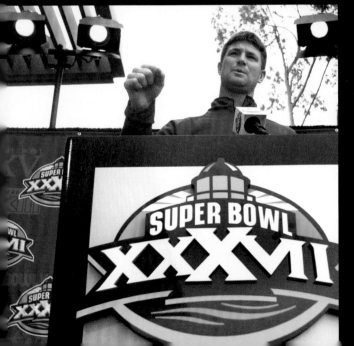

> Back in Black Mountain, I'm honored by a downtown parade. I have some fun dancing at the gym ceremony, where Mom and I are all smiles standing on stage. This picture of Max and me was on the field just after our Super Bowl win.

That night at our team hotel, true believers surrounded me. My family, parents, sister, best friend Nick Gonatos, long-time personal trainer Alex, my agents Phil Williams and Brian Lammi and business manager Rochelle Johnson were all there to celebrate.

Also there were two special guests I flew in for the game—Kenny Ford and Bill Burrows—my high school football and basketball coaches.

After hours of hugs, backslapping, and laughter, I went to bed wearing my jersey. I was up before the sun for East Coast TV shows that started a whirlwind of activities and victory parades.

FUN FACT >>> BRAD HAS WORN NO. 14 THROUGH HIS HIGH SCHOOL, COLLEGE, AND PROFESSIONAL CAREER. BRAD CHOSE NO. 14 BECAUSE DAN FOUTS WAS HIS FAVORITE QUARTERBACK AND BOB COUSY WAS HIS FAVORITE BASKETBALL PLAYER. BOTH WORE NO. 14.

Tampa Bay fans welcomed us home with open arms and a hero's welcome. They lined the streets and filled our stadium to share in Tampa's first NFL championship. They waited 26 years and their passion poured out.

Seeing such excitement makes you realize how many people are touched by sports.

My hometown of Black Mountain held a parade for me a few months after the Super Bowl.

People from all over the Swannanoa Valley showed up on a crystal-blue-sky Sunday afternoon. I had never seen Black Mountain (population 7,500) full of so many people. They lined State Street as we drove through town and then to the high school.

Everyone packed the Owen High School gym and a number of people said a lot of nice things about me. I was very humbled. They even named a street after me.

The warm turnout really hit home as far as what it meant to me to go down in history as a Super Bowl winning quarterback. Many friends said they felt like they were in the Super Bowl with me. When you do something great, or just live a good life, it reflects back on everyone who helped you along your journey.

Many young students were there. I told them this simple message:

"MY CREED IN LIFE IS TO NEVER HAVE ANY REGRETS. FOR ME, I WILL HAVE NO REGRETS, AND I CHALLENGE YOU TO THAT."

Accomplishing your goal once is great. But you can't stop there. You have to set new sights. Coach Gruden tells us winning a Super Bowl once is greatness, doing it again is legendary.

BRAD JOHNSON WAY

Fan expectations were high for a Super Bowl repeat when the 2003 season opened.

Not many NFL teams repeat as champions. As a team we talked about winning it all again at our ring ceremony in June, but after that it was back to our daily business of improving each day.

WE ALL REALIZED "THE TRAIN KEEPS MOVING" AND THE NEW SEASON WOULD BE DIFFERENT. NOBODY KNEW HOW DIFFERENT IT WOULD BE.

We played well at times, but the season crumbled down the stretch. We had breakdowns on all sides of the ball, offense, defense, and kicking. We finished 7-9 and missed the playoffs.

The ball didn't bounce our way. We lost seven games by seven points or fewer, including two overtime games. Why? Injuries, distractions, mistakes, and bad luck all contributed. We lost six offensive starters to injury, and we set a team record for most penalties in a season.

It's easy to point fingers when things go wrong. In the end, there's only the mirror. You have to look in it and ask, "Did I prepare well? Did I try my best? Did I play with passion?"

Numbers placed me among the top five quarterbacks for the year in key categories, but I made my share of mistakes.

Before the next Super Bowl, there were questions about whether the Bucs were shopping for a new quarterback.

FUN FACT >>> DURING HIS NFL CAREER BRAD HAS WORKED WITH MANY CHARITIES, INCLUDING: THE RONALD MCDONALD HOUSE CHARITIES®, EBLEN CHARITIES, MAKE A WISH FOUNDATION®, AND BRAD'S READING CHAMPIONS.

Whatever people say about me, I don't let it affect my desire. I compare myself to a duck swimming. Above water ducks appear to glide smoothly. Underwater, their webbed feet are churning.

I'm the same way. On the outside I might look calm, but inside my passion is burning.

It's terrible when a person loses passion and gives up. Soon they don't care about family, don't care about learning, don't care about improving, don't care about the future or themselves.

Never put yourself in a position to look back and say, "I wish I'd tried harder."

That will never happen if you play with passion.

> I wear two pieces of white tape around the ring finger of my left hand during football games. It's not because my fingers are injured. It's one way I say "I love you" to Mom.

YEARLY RECORDS
FOR THE
TAMPA BAY
BUCCANEERS

	Reg. Season				Conf. Playoffs			
Year	W	L	T	Pct.	Pos.	W	L	Pct.	Playoff Summary
'76	0	14	0	.000	(5th)	—	—	—	—
'77	2	12	0	.143	(5th)	—	—	—	—
'78	5	11	0	.313	(5th)	—	—	—	—
'79	10	6	0	.625	(1st)	1	1	.50	Bye, Beat Philadelphia, Lost to LA Rams
'80	5	10	1	.344	(4th)	—	—	—	—
'81	9	7	0	.563	(1st)	0	1	.00	Bye, Lost to Dallas
'82	5	4	0	.556	(3rd)	0	1	.00	Lost to Dallas
'83	2	14	0	.143	(5th)	—	—	—	—
'84	6	10	0	.375	(3rd)	—	—	—	—
'85	2	14	0	.143	(5th)	—	—	—	—
'86	2	14	0	.143	(5th)	—	—	—	—
'87	4	11	0	.267	(4th)	—	—	—	—
'88	5	11	0	.313	(3rd)	—	—	—	—
'89	5	11	0	.313	(5th)	—	—	—	—
'90	6	10	0	.375	(2nd)	—	—	—	—
'91	3	13	0	.188	(5th)	—	—	—	—
'92	5	11	0	.313	(3rd)	—	—	—	—
'93	5	11	0	.313	(5th)	—	—	—	—
'94	6	10	0	.375	(5th)	—	—	—	—
'95	7	9	0	.438	(5th)	—	—	—	—
'96	6	10	0	.375	(4th)	—	—	—	—
'97	10	6	0	.625	(2nd)	1	1	.50	Beat Detroit, Lost to Green Bay
'98	8	8	0	.500	(3rd)	—	—	—	—
'99	11	5	0	.688	(1st)	1	1	.50	Beat Washington, Lost to St. Louis
'00	10	6	0	.625	(2nd)	0	1	.00	Lost to Philadelphia
'01	9	7	0	.563	(3rd)	0	1	.00	Lost to Philadelphia
'02	12	4	0	.750	(1st)	3	0	1.00	Beat San Fran, Philadelphia, Oakland (Super Bowl Champions)
'03	7	9	0	.438	(3rd)	—	—	—	—

ALL-TIME CAREER PASSING COMPLETION PERCENTAGE

(Minimum 3,000 attempts)

1	Steve Young	64.28
2	Joe Montana	63.24
3	Peyton Manning	62.90
4	Brad Johnson	61.77
5	Troy Aikman	61.46
6	Brett Favre	61.26
7	Mark Brunell	60.27
8	Jim Kelly	60.14
9	Ken Stabler	59.85
10	Danny White	59.69

HOW QUARTERBACKS MEASURE UP

NFL
Quarterback Rating Formula

The NFL rates its passers for statistical purposes against a fixed performance standard based on statistical achievements of all qualified pro passers since 1960.

Four categories are used as a basis for compiling a rating:
1. Percentage of completions per attempt
2. Average yards gained per attempt
3. Percentage of touchdown passes per attempt
4. Percentage of interceptions per attempt

The average standard is 1.000. The bottom is .000. To earn a 2.000 rating, a passer must perform at exceptional levels. In order to make the rating more understandable, the point rating is then converted into a scale of 100. In rare cases, where statistical performance has been superior, it is possible for a passer to surpass a 100 rating.

For example, take Steve Young's record-setting season in 1994 when he completed 324 of 461 passes for 3,969 yards, 35 touchdowns, and 10 interceptions.

The four calculations would be:

1. Percentage of Completions—324 of 461 is 70.28 percent. Subtract 30 from the completion percentage (40.28) and multiply the result by 0.05. The result is a point rating of 2.014.
Note: If the result is less than zero (Completion Percentage less than 30.0), award zero points. If the results are greater than 2.375 (Completion Percentage greater than 77.5), award 2.375.

2. Average Yards Gained Per Attempt—3,969 yards divided by 461 attempts is 8.61. Subtract three yards from yards-per-attempt (5.61) and multiply the result by 0.25. The result is 1.403.
Note: If the result is less than zero (Yards per Attempt less than 3.0), award zero points. If the result is greater than 2.375 (Yards per Attempt greater than 12.5), award 2.375 points.

3. Percentage of Touchdown Passes—35 touchdowns in 461 attempts is 7.59 percent. Multiply the touchdown percentage by 0.2. The result is 1.518.
Note: If the result is greater than 2.375 (Touchdown Percentage greater than 11.875), award 2.375.

4. Percentage of Interceptions—10 interceptions in 461 attempts is 2.17 percent. Multiply the interception percentage by 0.25 (0.542) and subtract the number from 2.375. The result is 1.833.
Note: If the result is less than zero (Interception Percentage greater than 9.5), award zero points.

The sum of the four steps is (2.014 + 1.403 + 1.518 + 1.833) 6.768. The sum is then divided by six (1.128) and multiplied by 100. In this case, the result is 112.8. This same formula can be used to determine a passer rating for any player who attempts at least one pass.

LEADING NFL LIFETIME PASSERS

- Minimum 1500 attempts
- Stats taken at start of 2004 season

Rank	Player	Yrs	Att	Comp	Yds	TD	INT	Rating
1	Kurt Warner	6	1,688	1,121	14,447	102	65	97.2
2	Steve Young	15	4,149	2,667	33,124	232	107	96.8
3	Joe Montana	15	5,391	3,409	40,551	273	139	92.3
4	Jeff Garcia	5	2,360	1,449	16,408	113	56	88.3
5	Peyton Manning	6	3,383	2,128	24,885	167	110	88.1
6	Daunte Culpepper	5	1,843	1,160	13,881	90	63	88.0
7	Brett Favre	13	6,464	3,960	45,646	346	209	86.9
8	Dan Marino	17	8,358	4,967	61,361	420	252	86.4
9	Trent Green	6	2,266	1,336	17,016	106	65	86.1
10	Tom Brady	4	1,544	955	10,233	69	38	85.9
11	Mark Brunell	10	3,643	2,196	25,793	144	86	85.2
12	Rich Gannon	15	4,138	2,492	28,219	177	102	84.7
13	Jim Kelly	11	4,779	2,874	35,467	237	175	84.4
14	Brad Johnson	12	3,401	2,101	23,239	140	95	84.1
15	Steve McNair	9	3,180	1,884	22,637	132	83	84.1
16	Roger Staubach	11	2,958	1,685	22,700	153	109	83.4
17	Brian Griese	6	1,808	1,118	12,576	76	59	83.0
18	Neil Lomax	8	3,153	1,817	22,771	136	90	82.7
19	Sonny Jurgensen	18	4,262	2,433	32,224	255	189	82.6
20	Len Dawson	19	3,741	2,136	28,711	239	183	82.5

White = Players active in 2003 season

Index

Websites for Brad Johnson

Brad Johnson	www.bradjohnson14.com
Brad Johnson (team bio and stats)	www.buccaneers.com/team/playerdetail.aspx?player=Johnson,Brad,14
Children's Miracle Network	www.cmn.org
Florida State University	www.fsu.edu
Gillette Children's Hospital	www.gillettechildrens.org
Glazer Family Foundation	www.glazerfamilyfoundation.com
Muscular Dystrophy Association	www.mdausa.org
National Football League (NFL)	www.nfl.com
Super Bowl	www.superbowl.com
Tampa Bay Buccaneers	www.buccaneers.com
Official NFL site for kids	www.playfootball.com